COMETS,
ASTEROIDS,
and METEORITES

Planet Guides

COMETS, ASTEROIDS, and METEORITES

Duncan Brewer

MARSHALL CAVENDISH
NEW YORK · LONDON · TORONTO · SYDNEY

Reference Edition Published 1993

© Marshall Cavendish Corporation 1992

Published by Marshall Cavendish Corporation
2415 Jerusalem Avenue
PO Box 587
North Bellmore
New York 11710

Series created by Graham Beehag Book Design

Library of Congress Cataloging-in-Publication Data

Brewer, Duncan, 1938-
    Comets, asteroids, and meteorites / Duncan Brewer.
     p. cm. – (Planet guides)
    Includes index.
    Summary: Examines the physical characteristics and conditions of comets, asteroids, and meteorites, describing their posituion and movements in relation to the sun and planets and surveying humanity's attempts to penetrate their mysteries.
    ISBN 1-85435-330-6 (set) . ISBN 1-85435-376-4
    i. Comets – Juvenile literature. 2. Asteroids – Juvenile literature.
    3. Meteorites – Juvenile literature. [1. Comets. 2. Asteroids.
    3. Meteorites.] I. Title. II. Series: Brewer, Duncan, 1938-
    Planet Guides.
    GB721.5.B74 1990   90-40813
                                       CIP
                                       AC

Printed in Malaysia by Times Offset Pte Ltd

SAFETY NOTE

Never look directly at the Sun, either with the naked eye or with binoculars or a telescope. To do so can result in permanent blindness.

Acknowledgement

Most of the photographs, maps and diagrams in this book have been kindly supplied by NASA.

Title Page Picture:

The comet Kohoutak photographed from Skylab 4. This is a false color image showing the comet's tail. The tail shows the dust, and possibly oxygen or other gases blown out of the comet by the solar wind.

Contents

Space Debris

The nine planets that orbit the Sun make up the Solar System. They are held in position by the gravity of the Sun. The Sun also holds on to a collection of space debris, lumps of rock and metal of varying sizes called *asteroids*, and *meteoroids*, and "frozen snowballs" of dust and gas called *comets*. Dust particles from comets sometimes enter the Earth's atmosphere and burn up. These are *meteors*, or shooting stars. Occasionally a larger chunk of rock or metal fails to burn up and crashes to Earth. Such an invader from space is called a *meteorite*.

Most known asteroids are found in the Asteroid Belt. Like the planets, they orbit the Sun. The total mass of all known asteroids amounts to about one two-thousandths of the mass of the Earth.

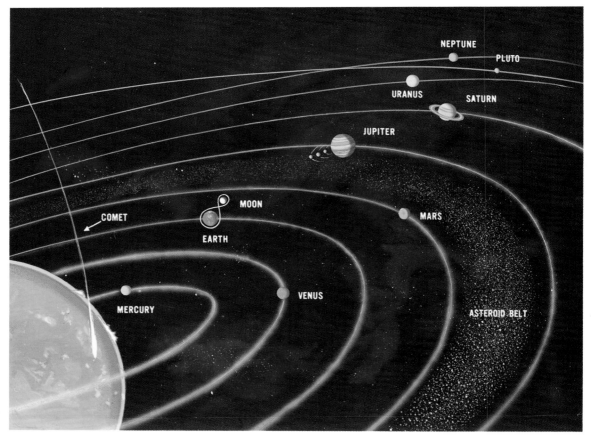

Cosmic Building Materials

The rocks, dust and gas of which asteroids, meteoroids and comets are composed are the materials of which the planets themselves are made. The Solar System was formed some 4,600,000,000 years ago from a gigantic cloud of dust and gas. This cloud was pulled inward by its own gravity and a star was formed. The rest of the cloud circled the new-born Sun. The dust particles collided and clung to each other, forming larger and larger lumps. The largest of the lumps, "mopping up" more and more clumps of particles,

Comet Ikeya-Seki was particularly brilliant when it was seen from Earth's southern hemisphere briefly in 1965. Discovered by two Japanese amateurs, it came very close to the Sun.

became the planets. Some were composed mostly of rock and metal, others mostly of gas. Most of the spare gas disappeared into space but the planets' gravity held on to some to give them atmospheres. As well as atmospheres, some of the planets captured satellites – rocky moons, or dust rings – that orbit them as they orbit the Sun.

Some of the debris currently moving through the Solar System may once have been incorporated in a planet or moon that disintegrated. But much of it has simply never been kidnapped by a larger body. It remains as it was the day the Solar System was born.

Pioneer 10 passed through the Asteroid Belt on its way to Jupiter. In this artist's impression, the five outermost planets of the Solar System are shown together with their orbits round the Sun. The Sun is shown in the middle distance with the planets on the far side of the Solar System. To make it easier to identify the planets, the Sun is shown much smaller than it would be at this scale. Pioneer 10 survived the dangers of crashing into the space debris of the Asteroid Belt to continue its epic journey beyond our own Solar System.

Asteroids

In March, 1989, an unknown asteroid, 1,000 feet (300 meters) across, came within 500,000 miles (800,000 kilometers) of Earth. In galactic terms, this is close enough to be considered a cat's whisker away from collision. No one saw the gigantic rock skim by, as it must have passed through a daytime sky. Skywatchers at California's Mount Palomar Observatory first noticed it on a sky-film taken in the first week of April. On this film, the object was moving away from Earth, but was still only 650,000 miles (1,000,000 kilometers) distant.

Too Close for Comfort

Calculations of the asteroid's speed and trajectory indicated that it had been closest to Earth on March 23, two weeks before the film was taken. Its orbit around the

Compared with planets and moons, most asteroids are relatively small. However, many are still huge in Earth terms. A number of asteroids are larger than major cities such as New York or London.

Sun will bring it past Earth again in 25 to 30 years. The close brush with our planet has probably accelerated the asteroid, so its next approach to Earth may be an even longer time away. That is good news, since a rock 1,000 feet (300 meters) across colliding with Earth could have disastrous effects.

The asteroid of March 1989, was large, previously unknown, and very close. It was just one of the billions of asteroids. The largest of these heavenly bodies, Ceres, discovered in 1801, has a diameter of about 625 miles (1,000 kilometers).

Spacecraft heading for the outer planets have to pass through the Asteroid Belt. Despite the fact that the belt is made up of millions of orbiting bodies, no spacecraft has so far suffered impact damage while traveling through it.

Discovering the Asteroids

In 1801, an Italian monk called Giuseppe Piazza found a new planet. He named it Ceres. The planet which orbits 2·77AU (*Astronomical Units* the Earth's average distance from the Sun) from the Sun, was small and dim. It was a mere 625 miles (1,000 kilometers) in diameter and its mass was a hundredth of that of our Moon. Was it really a planet?

In the following years, more similar but smaller bodies were discovered. Pallas was spotted in 1802,

When astronomers take time-lapse photographs of the stars, asteroids and other fast-moving bodies appear as streaks on the photographic plates.

Juno in 1804, and Vesta in 1807. Their diameters were 378 miles (608 kilometers), 155 miles (250 kilometers) and 334 miles (538 kilometers) respectivly. The four asteroids all orbited between the orbits of Mars and Jupiter.

The astronomer, William Herschel, who had discovered Uranus in 1781, coined the word asteroid for the new discoveries. Although they are small compared with the planets, asteroids behave exactly like planets, moving in regular, predictable orbits around the Sun. For this reason, they are often called *planetoids* or *minor planets*.

Photographing the Asteroid Belt

No more asteroids were discovered for nearly forty years until, in 1845, Astraea was first seen. It has a diameter of 73 miles (117 kilometers) and counts as one of the larger asteroids.

Around the turn of the century, astronomers started to use photography in their work, and they discovered many asteroids in the zone now known as the Asteroid Belt between the orbits of Mars and Jupiter. A German astronomer called Max Wolf swept the skies with a photographic telescope that turned at the same rate as the stars appear to revolve around the Earth, and thereby avoiding the blurring effect of the stars apparent motion. New asteroids were registered at amazing speed.

By 1989, some 4,044 asteroids had been listed, but they probably represent only a fraction of the total number. Hundreds of thousands of rocky bodies, from pebble-size up to the 625-mile (1,000-kilometer) bulk of Ceres, orbit within the belt, with as many as 400,000 with a diameter of over a ½ mile. Most are under 12½ miles (20 kilometers) in diameter. It has been estimated that about 100,000 asteroids, with a minimum diameter of 1½ miles (2½ kilometers), comprise the belt. About 200 of them are larger than 60 miles (95 kilometers) across; only 17 are known to have diameters larger than 140 miles (225 kilometers).

Jupiter's Companions

In addition to the asteroids in the Asteroid Belt, which orbit the sun at average distances between 2·2 and 3·3 AU, there are a handful of known independent wanderers with unusual orbits.

The asteroid Hidalgo has an orbit that varies

from 185,000,000 miles (300,000,000 kilometers) to 900,000,000 miles (1,450,000,000 kilometers) from the Sun. Chiron, the farthest known asteroid from the Sun, orbits between the orbits of Saturn and Uranus. There are also two groups sharing Jupiter's orbit, known as the Trojan Asteroids. The Trojans orbit in two groups, one group in front of Jupiter, and Jupiter's other trailing it. These two positions, known as Jupiter's

An artist's impression of the asteroid Icarus during its close approach to the Sun.

Lagrangian points, represent regions of stability, free from disruption by Jupiter's massive gravity field.

Earth Grazers

Some asteroids with extremely *eccentric orbits* come quite close to Earth. The asteroids of the *Apollo* group approach closer to the Sun than our own planet when they are at *perihelion*. There are 29 of them, named after an asteroid with a diameter of just over 1¼ miles (2 kilometers), which was discovered in 1932. Apollo is so small that it was "lost" after its discovery and only rediscovered again in 1973.

The Pioneer 10 and 11 space probes passed through the Asteroid Belt, which is about 125,000,000 miles (200,000,000 kilometers) across and 62,000,000 miles (100,000,000 kilometers) thick. The belt is so large that individual asteroids of significant size are millions of miles apart.

Did You Know?

Some scientists suggest that an asteroid may have collided with Earth 65,000,000 years ago, causing such dramatic changes in the climate that the dinosaurs were unable to survive the conditions and died out.

The Amor asteroids also come close to Earth at their perihelia, though their orbits pass outside our planet's path. There are more than 16 of them, and, like the Apollo group, they are all quite small. Amor, after which the group is named, was also discovered in 1932. It is less than half a mile (1 kilometer) across.

Most asteroids, seem to have originated from the breakup of larger bodies in the main Asteroid Belt. About 20 percent may be the nuclei of comets that have gradually disintegrated. Amor and Apollo asteroids are also known as Earth Grazing Asteroids (EGAs). A small number, called *binary asteroids,* have satellites of their own.

Perilous Orbits

The EGAs do not have stable orbits, but are constantly being shifted slightly from their paths by the gravitational pulls of Earth, Mars, and Venus. The cumulative effect of these strong pulls can send an asteroid coursing permanently out of its regular orbit to other parts of the Solar System. Alternatively, it can be set on a course that brings it close to a planet. If it gets close enough, it can be dragged by gravity down through the atmosphere, to crash into the planet's surface.

It is likely that the craters that pock-mark the faces of the Moon, Mercury and Mars were caused by EGA impacts. Constant geological activity and the effects of wind and rain have smoothed the surface of the Earth, eradicating all but a few impact craters. Scientists believe that eventually any asteroid in an Earth-grazing orbit will either be ejected from its orbit, or will crash down to the surface of one of the planets.

On the Asteroid Track

Modern photographic techniques, plus the heat-imaging capabilities of the Infrared Astronomical Satellite (IRAS), help find new asteroids every year. Rules of official cataloging are strict, and only about 4,000 have been registered so far. To join the list, an asteroid must be studied closely enough to establish its orbit, so that its movements can be accurately predicted for several years into the future.

The majority of asteroids are dark, reflecting only about 6 percent of sunlight falling on them. Known as C-type bodies, they are thought to have a similar composition to *carbonaceous meteorites*, containing carbon compounds. Brighter asteroids, with up to 25 percent reflectivity, are known as S-type. Most have a reddish color, and their spectra, analyzed with the aid of a *spectrograph*, indicate that they have a common silicate or stony mineral composition. C-type asteroids are found in their heaviest concentrations in the outer part of the Asteroid Belt, while there are slightly more S-types at the belt's inner margin.

Volcanic Vesta

Brightest of all the asteroids, with a reflectivity of 30 percent, is Vesta, which was discovered in 1807. Vesta is the third largest known asteroid, with a diameter of over 334 miles (538 kilometers). However, Vesta's main claim to fame is the fact that of all the known asteroids, it is the only one showing signs on its surface of previous volcanic activity. Vesta sits in the middle of the Main Belt. Its spectrum shows clear indications of rocks such as basalt which forms from volcanic lava. No other asteroid has revealed a similar composition.

Because of its surface basalts, Vesta is thought to be the source of a class of meteorites known as the *eucrites*. About thirty eucrite meteorites are known, and all of them seem to have come from the same parent body. They were probably blasted away from the basaltic surface of Vesta by a meteorite impact.

The Hidden Belt

Some astronomers believe that there is an outer asteroid belt, beyond the gas giants, and that Pluto, the ninth planet, is a part of it. Certainly it is possible to consider Pluto an asteroid instead of a true planet. It is much smaller than any other planet, and it is completely unrelated to the other outer planets. It has the most eccentric planetary orbit, as well as the most steeply inclined orbit. Some scientists feel that Pluto and its moon Charon could be a part of a possible outer asteroid belt.

16

Meteorites

If the 1,000-foot (300-meter) asteroid that grazed Earth in March, 1989, had been snared by Earth's gravity and pulled into the planet, it would have become a meteorite. A meteorite is an extraterrestrial body that survives the intense heat of atmospheric entry to reach the Earth's surface.

Asteroids and comets are plotted, named, and registered by astronomers, and they have predictable orbits. Meteoroids, on the other hand, are detected only when they enter the Earth's atmosphere. Meteoroid is the name given to interplanetary fragments ranging in size from specks of dust to miles-wide rock masses that are, in fact, destabilized asteroids.

A meteor is a small fragment of material, usually from dust granule to pea-sized, which can be seen on a clear night. Meteors, also known as "shooting stars," leave brief smears of *incandescence* across the sky as they burn up in the upper atmosphere.

The Leonid meteor shower occurs in the middle of November each year. This picture was taken from a mountaintop in Arizona, in November, 1966. That year saw a particularly rich meteor shower, with an estimated 1,000 meteors a minute over a period of 40 minutes.

Meteors on Schedule

Sometimes, Earth experiences the cosmic fireworks display of a *meteor shower*. Minor meteor showers occur every year, reappearing regularly on particular dates. Every August, for example, between the 9th and 13th of the month, the Perseid shower makes its display in the northern night sky. The Perseids are named after the constellation of Perseus, as they appear to come from

Major meteor showers do not occur every year. This one, the Leonids, was viewed off Cape Florida, in 1799. The next major shower did not occur until 1833.

that direction. Other regular meteor showers include the Draconids, which peak in intensity on October 9; the Orionids on October 20; the Leonids, on November 16; and the Geminids on December 13.

Death of a Comet

The explanation for meteor showers became evident in 1872, when a brilliant meteor shower occurred at the time a comet should have been passing overhead. The Comet Biela had been discovered in 1826 and was calculated to reappear every 6 years and 9 months. To the amazement of the sky-watchers in 1846, Biela seemed to be splitting into two. The next time it appeared, in 1852, both parts visited Earth together,

The meteors from a meteor shower appear to travel across the night sky from a point known as the radiant. In this nineteenth-century illustration, the Leonid shower meteors appear to come from the direction of the constellation Leo. In fact, it is the Earth's movement into the path of the meteors that creates this impression.

Major Annual Meteor Showers

Shower	Duration	Max	Associated Comet
Quadrantids	Jan 1-6	Jan 3	?
Lyrids	April 19-24	April 22	Thatcher 1861
Eta Aquarids	May 2-7	May 4	Halley
Delta Aquarids	July 15-Aug 15	July 28	?
Perseids	July27-Aug 18	Aug 12	Swift-Tuttle
Orionids	Oct 16-26	Oct 21	Halley
Taurids	Oct 26-Nov 25	Nov 4	Encke
Leonids	Nov 15-19	Nov 17	Tempel-Tuttle
Geminids	Dec 7-15	Dec 14	?

about 2,000,0000 miles (3,200,000 kilometers) apart. Nothing else was seen of Biela until the appointed time in 1872. Then, instead of a comet, a brilliant meteor shower filled the sky. The Earth was passing through the orbit of the now extinct comet, which had become an orbiting stream of cosmic dust particles.

Annual Interception

We now know that the annual meteor showers occur

The great daylight bolide of August 10, 1972, photographed from the Grand Teton National Park, Wyoming. The meteor which had an estimated weight of 1,000,000 tons, burned in Earth's atmosphere for 101 seconds. It was traveling at 33,000 mph (53,000 km/h) and its closest approach to Earth was 36 miles (58 kilometers).

21

regularly because the Earth intercepts the orbits of certain comets at precisely the same time each year. Some of these comets are not yet defunct, but have shed a great deal of material into their orbits.

When a meteor shower occurs, the meteors seem to spread out toward us. They appear to come from a fixed point when they are seen from Earth. The fixed

point is called the *radiant*, and the apparent spreading out is just a trick of perspective – an optical illusion – as Earth heads directly into the streaming particles.

Ancient Displays

Some historical meteor showers have been truly spectacular. A great shower in 1899 produced a display of 100,000 meteors an hour, as Earth forged its way through an especially thick segment of the orbit of Comet Tempel-Tuttle. Historical records of this regular shower, which is not always as dense as it was in 1899,

Most meteors are seen for only a fraction of a second, but occasionally, a bright specimen travels right across the sky for several seconds. This one was seen near London in 1850. Particularly bright meteors, known as bolides, can sometimes be seen in daylight, when molten material from the tail appears as a white trail against the sky.

go back as far as the seventh century B.C. Known as the Lyrids, it occurs every April 21. There are also accounts of the Perseids going back to 36 A.D., and the Delta Aquarids can be dated back to 401 A.D.

In all, there are about two dozen showers that appear regularly each year. Nearly all are associated with comets, active or dead. However, the Geminids, which appear in mid-December, are associated with a small asteroid, Phaeton, one of the Apollo family. Phaeton is probably the rocky core of a comet still locked in an orbit rich with particles from its old mantle.

Single meteor streaks are known as sporadic meteors. They come from a variety of sources, including dispersed meteor streams, material ejected by the impact of meteorites, and collisions with asteroids.

Meteor-Trail Radio

Literally millions of meteors burn up in Earth's upper atmosphere every 24 hours, though only a very small number are seen by observers on the ground. Radio scientists have developed a way to take advantage of this constant bombardment. Every meteor leaves in its wake a trail of *ionized gases* at altitudes of between 40 and 70 miles (70 and 110 kilometers). By bouncing radio waves off these trails, it is possible to send VHF radio signals up to 1,500 miles (2,400 kilometers) away.

This technique is known as meteor-burst communication. The system is equipped with a constant probe beam which detects meteors in the right position. When the time is right, messages stored in the apparatus are fired off in ultra-fast bursts. Long-distance truckers far from base have been among the first users of meteor-burst technology, which gives them a communication range far beyond anything accessible to cellular phone systems.

Meteorites

The meteors we see are probably only about the size of a pea. Meteorites have to be considerably larger to survive the friction of Earth's atmosphere. Up to ten meteorites a day, each weighing more than 2 pounds (1 kilogram), hit our planet's surface, although they are generally not seen.

Space Invaders

There are three main groups of meteorites, distinguished by their different composition. Stones, or aeroliths, are stony meteorites consisting of silicates; a large proportion of them contain *chondrules*, sphere-shaped material not found on Earth. About a millimeter in diameter, they are formed from an aggregate of the silicates olivine and pyroxin. The stony meteorites are the most common group, forming about 65 percent of all meteorites found.

Irons, or siderites, are metallic meteorites made chiefly of iron and nickel. They represent about 35 percent of known meteorites.

The last 4 or 5 percent consists of the stony-irons, or sideroliths, which are half metallic and half silicate. Carbonaceous chondrites are rare stony meteorites.

Most meteorites come from material formed at the birth of the Solar System. However, a large carbonaceous chondrite named the Allende meteorite, which shattered when it landed in Mexico in 1969, contains white material that appear to date from before the formation of the Solar System.

The Ahnighito or Tent, meteorite, seen here chained to a wagon for transportation, was discovered in Greenland in the late nineteenth century. It weighed 66,100 pounds (30,000 kilograms) and is now displayed at New York's American Museum of Natural History. The Eskimos who lived near where it landed, made metal harpoon heads from smaller fragments of the meteorite.

A large meteorite which fell in Brazil in 1887 was recovered with the aid of a special truck on rails. The very largest meteorites, some weighing more than 20 tons, all consist mainly of nickel-iron.

Hot Entry

Earth's gravitational pull strengthens as objects get nearer to the planet's surface. At the top of the planet's atmosphere, a meteorite hurtles at a speed of many miles a second. It begins to heat up from the friction caused by its journey. As the meteorite gets closer, it also gets faster. The friction intensifies as the atmosphere becomes denser.

At an altitude of about 62 miles (100 kilometers), the meteorite glows with incandescence as its surface melts. The atmosphere along its path also lights up in

Did You Know?

On August 10, 1972, a meteorite estimated to be 265 feet (80 meters) across entered the Earth's atmosphere. It came within 36 miles (58 kilometers) of the planet's surface and then left the atmosphere again, heading out into solar orbit at an increased speed.

the intense heat. It forms a glowing tail many times larger than the meteorite itself, as drops of molten material begin to stream from the rear of the meteorite, forming a white trail in daylight. This process, called *ablation*, usually destroys most of the meteorite before it strikes the Earth. In fact, most smaller bodies melt away completely before they reach Earth's surface.

As a meteorite travels through the lower atmosphere, the tremendous buildup of air pressure causes *sonic booms* and shockwaves which put great stress on its structure. Many meteorites, particularly the stony ones, break into fragments before landing.

This fanciful seventeenth-century woodcut portrays a shower of meteorite fragments in England in 1628 as a heavenly artillery battle. Such displays occur when a large meteorite breaks up before impact.

Did You Know?

Meteorites provided some of the first readily accessible iron used by man. This iron may have been an important contribution to the transition from the Bronze Age to the Iron Age.

Meteorite Noise

Observers on Earth see the arrival of a meteorite as a fiery streak at night and a bright, vaporous trail during daylight. The brightest fireballs, usually associated with large bodies, are called *bolides*. They are often heard as well as seen, emitting thunderous roars, sonic booms, and sparkling crackles. Within a range of about 30 miles (50 kilometers), they may create rushing and whistling noises in the final stages.

In the last stages of descent, at an altitude of around 5 miles (8 kilometers), the friction may become so great, depending on the angle of its path, that the meteorite is slowed down considerably. This can lower the temperature, extinguish the fireball, and allow the molten surface to solidify and survive its descent. Many meteorites break up before they land, and fragments may be strewn over a large area, usually in a roughly circular or oval shape.

Earth-fall

A meteorite tracked down after being observed is called a fall, whereas those discovered by chance are called finds. Most meteorites strike unnoticed and are never found because they land in the oceans or in remote, unpopulated areas.

Stony meteorites, the most common group, are much more difficult to find than the less frequent metallic ones. They merge into the landscape and are eroded by the weather until they are indistinguishable from local rock. The metallic meteorites are very heavy and are more distinctive in appearance. They do not suffer erosion to the same extent, and they can be found with magnets or metal-sensitive detectors. As a result, the majority of meteorites on display in museums are metallics.

Frozen Record

The Antarctic ice sheet is a rich source of meteorites in perfect condition. Slow-moving glaciers deposit meteorites, which may have fallen thousands of years earlier, near the surface, where wind erosion can reveal them. Scientists have recovered hundreds of interesting meteorites on the frozen continent. Because they have been protected from erosion by their long entombment in the ice, they are especially useful for research.

A few of the Antarctic meteorites are very similar in structure to material brought back by the astronauts

Left: Apollo 6 leaving the launch pad on April 4, 1968. Eventually astronauts from the Apollo Moon missions brought back rock samples from the Moon. Some of them closely resemble the material of meteorites that have been discovered in the Antarctic.

Below: This romantic depiction of a meteor and its tail was made in 1870. The tail of a meteor consists of heated atmospheric gases. They glow with incandescence caused by the friction of the meteor's swift flight through the Earth's atmosphere.

Unlike the Earth, the Moon is covered in meteorite impact craters that are immediately recognizable. Apollo 12 astronauts took this photograph of the crater Eratosthenes.

from the Apollo Moon missions. They may have been pieces of rock flung away from the Moon as the result of meteorite impacts on its surface. There are numerous impact craters that cover a large part of the lunar landscape.

Smooth Planet

The Earth has a greater gravity, so it drags more

material toward it than the Moon does. However, the Moon's lack of an atmosphere means that meteoroids approaching it do not burn up or break into fragments. Also, there is no wind or rain on the Moon to erode surface features, such as impact-craters, so the Moon has kept the record of its meteorite impacts clearly visible on its face. By comparison, hardly any impact craters are visible on Earth's surface.

Meteorite activity was far more intense in the early history of the Solar System than it is now. In the first 700,000,000 years, the planets and planetesimals (tiny planets), and many of their moons, grew by *accretion*, mopping up space debris until most of what was left orbited the Sun in the region of the Asteroid Belt.

Crater History

Some of the craters on our Moon are gigantic, almost 625 miles (1,000 kilometers) across, from the earliest period of meteorite bombardment. The average size of craters has gradually decreased. There is nothing on Earth to match the huge *mare basins* of the Moon, or the great craters of Mars, some of which are 1,100

Mariner 6 and 7 took high-resolution pictures of Mars in 1969, covering the most heavily cratered regions of the Martian terrain. The "Giant's Footprint" consists of two linked meteorite craters near the south pole of Mars.

miles (1,800 kilometers) across and 2½ miles (4 kilometers) deep. Earth must have been struck by meteorites of a similar size to those that struck the Moon and Mars, but most of the craters have long since disappeared, as the surface of the Earth has changed, as a rsult of geological activity and the effects of wind and rain.

Oldest Evidence

More than 120 impact craters have been discovered on Earth. Most were formed less than 200,000,000 years ago. The very largest are much older. A crater near Sudbury, Ontario, in Canada, had an original diameter of 90 miles (145 kilometers). It is about 1,800,000,000 years old. The only other known crater of that age is at Vredefort in South Africa.

Canada has a large proportion of Earth's surviving meteorite craters, though only one that old. A crater at

The huge meteorite that created the Barringer Crater in Arizona threw up a wall around itself. It ranges from 100 feet (30 meters) to 150 feet (45 meters) high.

Lake Manicouagan in Quebec is about 210,000,000 years old. It has filled with rainwater and now forms a lake with a diameter of 46 miles (74 kilometers). The meteorite that caused it must have had a diameter of nearly 2 miles (3 kilometers).

Arizona Impact

The most obvious large-scale craters surviving on Earth's surface come from relatively recent times in terms of Solar System history. Barringer Crater (also known inaccurately as Meteor Crater), in the Arizona desert, was created about 30,000 years ago by an iron meteorite calculated to have been 200 feet (60 meters) in diameter, with a mass of over a million tons.

The meteorite, traveling at about 10 miles (15 kilometers) a second when it landed, dug out a bowl-shaped crater with a raised rim. Barringer Crater is

This meteorite, kept in a dry nitrogen cabinet at the Johnson Space Center in Houston, was discovered in 1981 by an Antarctic meteorite recovery team and is thought possibly to have come from Mars.

4,000 feet (1,200 meters) across and has a visible floor 560 feet (170 meters) deep. Below this area is a lens-shaped layer of broken and jumbled rock fragments called *breccia*. The bottom of the breccia is about 1,250 feet (380 meters) below the crater's rim.

Physics of Self-Destruction

When a meteorite with a mass of more than 1,000 tons strikes the Earth at 15 miles (25 kilometers) a second, it creates phenomenal amounts of heat and pressure. Pressures of more than a million Earth atmospheres are combined with temperatures of thousands of degrees Celsius. The meteorite, together with much of the surface it strikes, is vaporized. Massive lumps of meteorite are found only where they have fragmented before impact.

Space Iron

The lump of nickel-iron that gouged out Barringer Crater is known as the Canyon Diablo meteorite. Although nothing remains of the main meteorite within the crater, tons of fragments have been discovered scattered within a 6-mile (10-kilometer) radius of the crater. The meteorite itself was melted and partially vaporized by the enormous force of the impact.

A meteorite found in Antarctica. It has characteristics very similar to rocks brought back from the highlands of the Moon. A section has been cut out for study and displays a selection of several minerals and an outer crust where the surface has melted during its fiery passage through the atmosphere.

The largest unbroken meteorite in the world is quite small compared to the ancient bodies that created some of the largest craters. The Hoba West Iron in Namibia, in southwestern Africa, has a mass around 60 tons, and dimensions of 9 by 9 by 3 feet (2·75 by 2·75 by 1 meter). It probably fell several thousand years ago, but there is no crater. The only logical explanation is that it must have approached the Earth at a very shallow angle, causing it to be slowed down much more than usual.

This meteor shower was observed in 1872, 1885 and 1892 when the Earth crossed the path of Biela's lost comet. The periodic comet, discovered in 1772, had a period of 6·6 years. When it reappeared in 1846, it had split in two.

Introduction to the Iron Age

The second-largest known meteorite weighs 30 tons and is also made of iron, as are all ten of the biggest meteorites. The Ahnighito, or Tent, meteorite fell a mere 10,000 years ago in Cape York, Greenland. It eventually became an object of wonder for Cape York Eskimos, who used fragments from the meteorite to make metal tips for their harpoons. It is now on display in the American Museum of Natural History in New York.

Every year, Earth's mass is increased by about 10,000 tons of meteorite material, most of it no larger than grains of sand. Meteorites large enough to produce dramatic fireballs are rare. Folk legends from across the world are full of tales of "thunder-stones" and other wondrous phenomena. Some large falls are well documented, though it was not until the beginning of the nineteenth century that it was generally accepted that meteorites came from beyond Earth's atmosphere.

Fireball in Siberia

On June 30, 1908, a massive meteorite explosion occurred several miles above the Earth's surface in Siberia. The huge fireball of this meteorite was seen for hundreds of miles before it exploded 6 miles (10 kilometers) above the Tunguska region. The explosion was heard 625 miles (1,000 kilometers) away and flattened trees in a 40-mile (60-kilometer) wide area.

The Largest Meteorites

Name	Location	Weight (tons)
Hoba West Iron	Namibia	60
Ahnighito (The Tent)	Greenland	31
Bacubirito	Mexico	27
Mbosi	Tanzania	26
Agpalilik	Greenland	20
Armanty	Outer Mongolia	20
Willamette	Oregon	14
Chupaderos	Mexico	14
Campo del Cielo	Argentina	13
Mundrabilla	Western Australia	12
Morito	Mexico	11

Despite the scale of the explosion, there was no crater because of the height of the burst. The only surviving traces of the Tunguska meteorite were minute spheres of molten meteorite material which have been found embedded in the spongy peat of the region.

Many scientists think that the Tunguska meteorite was a fragment of the Comet Encke. This comet is responsible for the Taurid meteor shower, which is visible at the end of October each year. It is gradually working its way closer to Earth's orbit and appears to be in the process of breaking up.

The Tunguska meteoritic explosion of 1908 leveled pine forests over a wide area, killed herds of reindeer, and was preceded by what was described as a descending shiny object brighter than the Sun, by observers 375 miles (600 kilometers) away from the center of the explosion.

Death of the Dinosaurs

Many scientists believe that a gigantic meteorite that fell to Earth 66,000,000 years ago may have been responsible for the extinction of many animal and plant species. The meteorite, which has been calculated to have had a diameter of 6¼ miles (10 kilometers), struck the planet at the end of the *Cretaceous Period*. At this time the dinosaurs suddenly became extinct. After dominating the Earth for millions of years, these great reptiles gave place to the tiny mammals that gained ascendancy during the *Tertiary Period* that followed.

Clay deposits from this time around the world contain an unusually high concentration of the element iridium.

This substance is rare on Earth, but abundant in meteorites, and it is thought to have been released and dissipated by the huge impact.

Deadly Cataclysm

The giant meteorite could have caused the extinction of species in a number of ways. If it landed in the ocean, it could have caused a *tsunami* (giant tidal wave) as high as 330 feet (100 meters). Some investigations have revealed layers of marine debris consistent with the passage of a giant wave at this time.

The impact would also have thrown a vast amount of material into the atmosphere. It could have blocked out the light of the Sun long enough to disrupt the growth of plants, and to disturb other life forms dependent on these plants. Scientists know that 70 percent of all the life on Earth was extinguished at about this time. The Cretaceous-Tertiary boundary also shows widespread fossil traces of soot, intense shock fractures in mineral grains, and spherules of molten rock. The crater of a meteorite on this scale would have been up to 25 miles (40 kilometers) deep. This depth would have been more than enough to penetrate oceanic and continental crusts, causing immense volcanic reactions and outpourings.

Some meteors can be seen exploding as they burn up high in the Earth's atmosphere. This one displayed three separate explosions before fading out.

Volcanic Trigger

Both the Sunbury, Canada, and Vredefort, South Africa, meteorite craters show evidence of having triggered volcanic eruptions. Large-scale volcanic activity would have contributed significantly to the extinction of many species. Widespread eruptions would have added to atmospheric dust, which might have led first to a period of permanent winter and then, eventually, to an equally traumatic global warming, complete with deadly *acid rain.*

It appears that a fairly modest asteroid colliding with Earth could destroy most life. Yet, it is also possible that meteorites may once have introduced to Earth the materials from which life was eventually born. Organic carbons and *amino acids*, the building blocks of life, have been found within the meteorites.

Built by NASA to assess meteoroid threats to spacecraft, the Meteoroid Technology Satellite was designed to collect data from its orbit close to the Earth.

In the nineteenth century, scientists sometimes used hot-air balloons to rise high enough above the clouds and haze to get a clear view of events in the night sky. This Leonid meteor shower was observed in 1870.

Below: This illustration from a Swiss book of 1557 depicts a meteorite falling to Earth.

Comets

The planetary region of the Solar System is only a tiny inner zone compared to the full extent of the Sun's influence. Far out beyond the orbits of the nine planets familiar to us, a great sphere, 200,000 AU across, defines the real outer limits. This is the *Oort Cloud*, which begins about 40,000 AU from the Sun and is the home of the comets.

Dirty Snowballs

Comets are ancient objects, formed in the outer reaches of the Solar System from the ice of gases such as methane, water vapor and ammonia, together with dust from primitive rock compounds. They are icy lumps, wandering icebergs sometimes described as "dirty snowballs."

In their "home" region of the Oort Cloud, comets are invisible to us, reflecting hardly any light. They are rela-

The Bayeux Tapestry portrays Halley's Comet soaring over the ill-fated King Harold before the Norman invasion of England. The English courtiers are shown marveling at the comet. People of the time saw the comet as an omen foretelling the English defeat at the Battle of Hastings.

tively tiny – just a few miles across on average – and tailless. These nuclei are very different from the glowing balls of light, with multimillion-mile-long tails, that occasionally visit the inner Solar System.

Rare Visitors

The sky does not teem with comets as it does with meteors. They cannot be seen every night, with or without a telescope. On average, Earth-bound observers can see one comet a year with the naked eye. Really

Halley's Comet has the longest recorded history of any comet. This picture shows the comet's appearance in 1456. Worried by the comet's reputation as a bringer of bad luck, Pope Calixtus III excommunicated it!

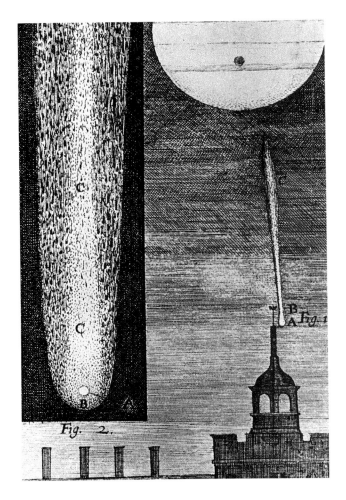

impressive comets, bright and long-tailed, only turn up about once every ten years.

Comets have inspired awe and fear throughout history and have been considered as warnings of the displeasure of the gods. The oldest written reference to a comet comes from China, in the fifteenth century B.C., and links its appearance with an official's treacherous murder of his supporters.

Warnings in the Sky

The Bayeux Tapestry, woven to commemorate William of Normandy's successful invasion of Britain in 1066, shows the English King Harold sitting on his throne as Halley's Comet streams overhead, foreshadowing his death on the battlefield.

Astrologers and prophets almost invariably saw comets as portents of disasters such as famines, plagues, and military defeats. Comets are said to have appeared

Above Left: In the seventeenth century, astronomers began to use telescopes to study comets. This one was observed in 1677 by Robert Hooke, an English scientist who may also have been the first man to record Jupiter's Great Red Spot.

The Great Comet of 1811 dominated the night sky. It is shown here as it appeared on October 15, from a hill near Winchester in England. The Great Comet is considered the largest ever recorded, with a coma diameter of 1,250,000 miles (2,000,000 kilometers), and a tail of over 100,000,000 miles (160,000,000 kilometers) long.

Famous Comets

	Orbital period	First seen
Encke's	3·3 years	1786
Pons-Winnecke	6·0 years	1819
Biela's	6·6 years	1772
Holmes'	6·85 years	1892
Schwassmann-Wachmann I	16·2 years	1925
Halley's	76 years	2400 BC?
Ikeya-Seki	880 years	1965
Donati's	2,040 years	1858
Humason's	2,900 years	1961
Arend-Roland	10,000 years	1957
Kohoutek's	75,000 years	1973

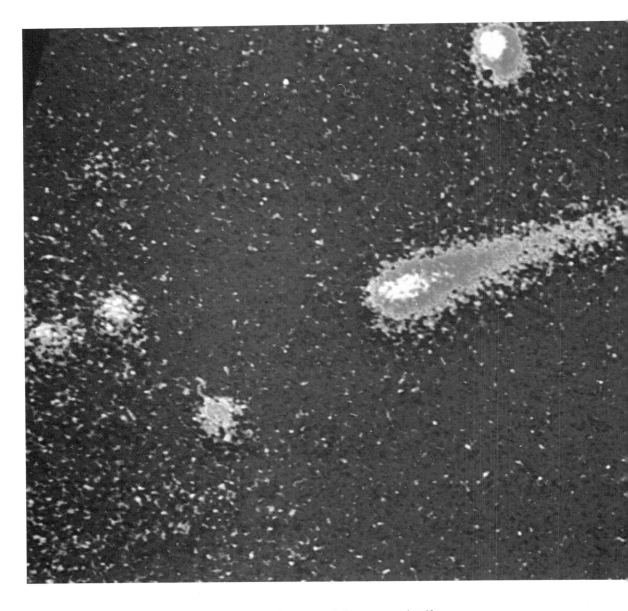

just before the deaths of such notables as Attila the Hun (AD 453), the Prophet Mohammed (AD 632), Richard the Lion-Heart (1198), and Napoleon (1821).

Slow Orbits

Circulating in the vastness of the Oort Cloud, up to 9,300,000,000,000 miles (15,000,000,000,000 kilometers) from the Sun, the comets slowly traverse great solar orbits that may take millions of years to complete. We would have no inkling of their existence except that, occasionally, they are dislodged from these

Comet Kohoutek is shown here in false-color to indicate different levels of brightness. It was photographed from Skylab in December 1973, against a background of the stars of the constellation Sagittarius.

orbits and sent swinging in toward the Sun on new, long, curving orbits.

The outer limits of the Oort Cloud are halfway to the nearest star (Proxima Centauri), and scientists think that the gravitational influence of passing stars may be a major cause of a comet's dislodgment. Some fall inward, toward the Sun, while others leave the Solar System for interstellar space.

Galactic Clouds

Comets may also be affected by other influences as the Solar System travels through the Milky Way Galaxy. In

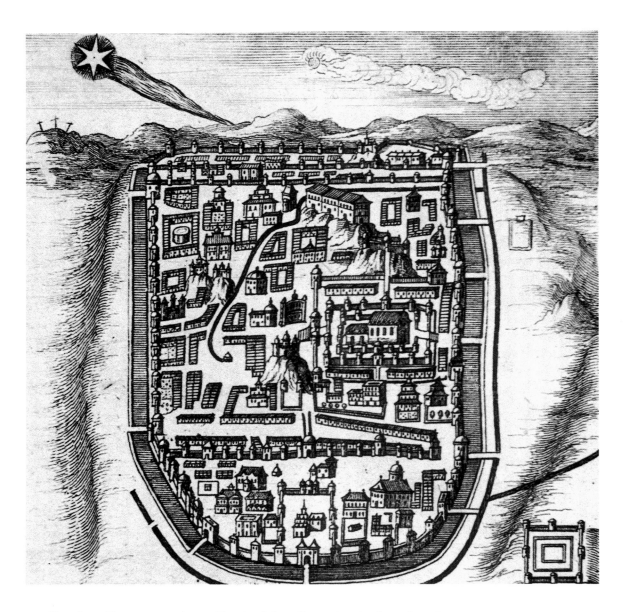

particular, they may be affected by the giant clouds of molecular hydrogen and other compounds, mixed with dust, that exist in the galaxy. These clouds are up to 300 times as dense as ordinary gases in space. They are 300 *light years* across, with a mass that could be a million times greater than that of the Sun.

Encounters with these clouds could cause radical disruptions to the Oort Cloud, jolting showers of comet nuclei out of their old orbits. Some scientists estimate that the Solar System has had up to 15 such encounters since its formation, each one resulting in comet-stripping from the outer regions.

This seventeenth century picture shows Halley's Comet passing over Jerusalem in A.D. 66. It has been viewed and recorded each time it reurns on it's 76-year orbit since 240 B.C. It may also have been the comet recorded by the Chinese observers in 1059 B.C.

Another cosmic effect that could dislodge comets is the galactic tides. These stem from the galaxy's own gravity, which pulls in alternate directions as the Solar System moves through space.

Heading for the Sun

A comet that begins the long journey from the Oort

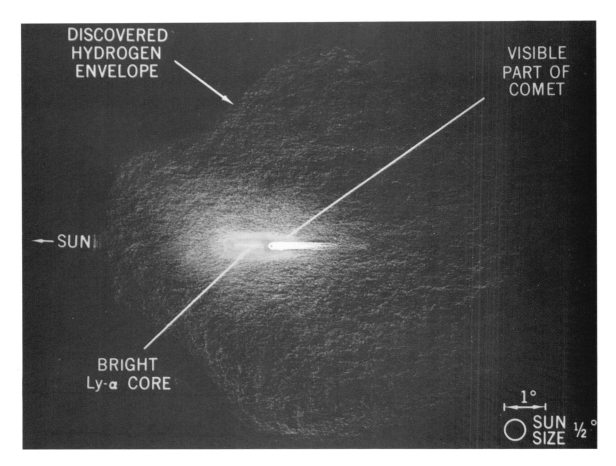

DISCOVERED
HYDROGEN
ENVELOPE

VISIBLE
PART OF
COMET

←SUN

BRIGHT
Ly-α CORE

1°

SUN
SIZE ½°

Cloud to the inner Solar System starts as a lump of dusty ice, unilluminated and tailless. It is traveling marginally faster than its previous 220 mph (350 km/h) orbital speed in the Oort Cloud. The extra speed comes from whatever gravitational nudge tipped it toward the Sun.

At this cosmic snail's pace, the comet takes a million years or more to come within sight of Earth. However, before it gets that far, some startling changes take place as the Sun's rays begin to have an effect. In the Oort Cloud, the comet's temperature was close to Absolute Zero ($-273.15°C$ or $-459.6°F$). At a distance of about 375,000,000 miles (600,000,000 kilometers) from the Sun, the solid, icy nucleus begins to give off gas and dust.

Lights On

The gas and dust given off collect in a roughly spherical cloud around the nucleus. At this point, the comet starts to be visible from Earth; some comets have a halo or

This illustration of Comet Bennet is based on ultraviolet images taken on April 1, 1970. The comet's atomic hydrogen envelope is enormous compared to the size of the visible comet. This hydrogen has been estimated to have a mass of about a million tons.

48

coma larger than the planet Jupiter. The dust in the cloud reflects the Sun's rays, which are absorbed and re-emitted at various wavelengths by the gases.

Ultraviolet light also reveals a huge, extremely thin, outer cloud of hydrogen, which extends outward to a diameter several times greater than that of the Sun.

Million-Mile Streamers

The thing that distinguishes comets from other heavenly bodies is their tails. Unlike a meteor, a comet does not trail a streamer of burning gases, for it does not enter the Earth's atmosphere. Out in the vacuum of space, there is no friction to create the heat that burns up meteors. Nor does a comet travel at anything like the speeds achieved by meteoroids.

Illustration of Brooks' Comet showing details of the tail. The background of stars appears streaked because of the long exposure. Photographers attempted to take pictures of comets as early as 1861, in the first years of photography, but had little success until the 1880s.

When you look at a comet in the sky, it does not appear to move. It may take weeks or even months for it to disappear from view. Anything you see moving swiftly across the sky cannot be a comet. A comet moves so slowly in relation to its distance from Earth that no motion is visible.

Two-Tailed Comets

The tail of a comet consists of material emanating from its coma. In fact, most comets have two tails, though

Below: Halley's Comet was studied intensively during its 1986 appearance. Five space probes attempted to approach close enough to photograph its nucleus. This image shows the trailing strands of Halley's plasma tail.

Four images, taken on August 22, 24, 26 and 27, 1957, show changes in the tails of the Comet Mrkos. The long, narrow tail is the gaseous plasma tail. The shorter, curving tail on the right consists of dust.

Images from July 9 and 10 and August 8, 1962, of Humason's Comet. This comet was too far from the Sun for the solar wind to be able to create a streaming tail.

Did You Know?
According to astronomers Chandra Wickramasinghe and Sir Fred Hoyle, life may have originated far out in space and been brought to Earth aboard a comet which crashed on the surface.

they are often in line with one another so that, from Earth's perspective, they appear as one. One long, thin tail consists of ionized gases, such as water vapor, carbon monoxide, nitrogen, and carbon dioxide. These long "plasma" tails have been calculated to be up to 200,000,000 miles (320,000,000 kilometers) in length. The other tail is a dust tail, which is shorter, wider, and less dense, and usually has a slight curve. The dust tail, which under infrared examination often reveals particles of

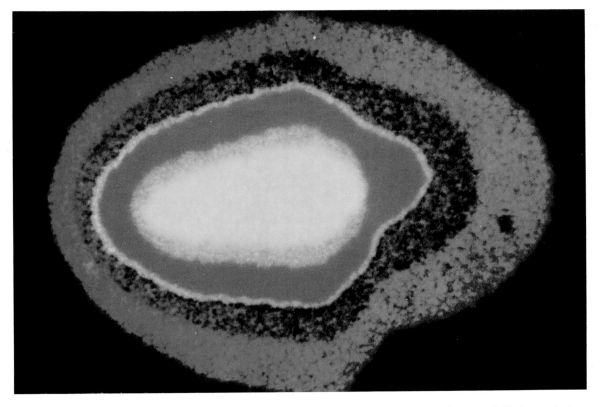

This picture, taken by the Infra-Red Astronomical Satellite (IRAS) in 1983 gives a heat image of a comet which came close to striking the Earth.

metallic silicates, shines with the reflected light of the Sun. The plasma tail is fluorescent, producing some of its own light, particularly the bluish light given out by ionized carbon monoxide.

Blowing in the Wind

The tail of a comet does not stream behind it, away from its direction of travel. The direction of the tail is determined by the solar wind, the swift and powerful flow of charged particles emanating from the Sun. The tail of a comet always points away from the Sun, pushed by the solar wind.

Snared by Gravity

Comets are divided into long-period types with orbits of more than 200 years, and short-period types with orbits of less than 200 years. All comets begin as long-period types, making the long journey from the Oort Cloud. They are then "captured" by the gravitational fields of the planets, particularly Jupiter, and transferred into new orbits around the Sun.

The long-period comets, which may have orbital periods of more than a million years, can have orbits at any angle, because they can come from any region of the Oort Cloud. Once they have been captured, however, they nearly all fall into line with the movement of the planets, staying close to the *ecliptic* and orbiting the Sun in the same direction as the planets. Halley's Comet, a short-period comet with an orbital period of about 76 years, is an exception. It has a *retrograde* orbit.

Bennett's Comet, photographed here in 1970, is named after the South African amateur astronomer who discovered it. Many amateurs specialize in searching for comets, and they discover more comets than professionals, whose equipment is taken up with other tasks.

Edmond Halley was a scientist of great note. It was he who persuaded Isaac Newton to write up the theory of gravitation, and even paid for the publication of the work himself. He was appointed Astronomer Royal at the age of 65 and spent 18 years working to understand the motion of the Moon. He died at the age of 86.

Halley's Comet

Halley's is the best known comet in the world. Edmond Halley, a colleague of Isaac Newton, was the first scientist to prove that comets could have periodic orbits that made their movements predictable.

In 1682, Halley saw the comet that was to be named after him. One of his many projects in the early years of the eighteenth century was to calculate the orbits of 24 comets from a multitude of sightings over the years. To do this, he used the work of Newton on the effects of planetary attraction on orbiting bodies.

Halley Gets it Right

Halley realized that the Great Comets of 1531, 1607,

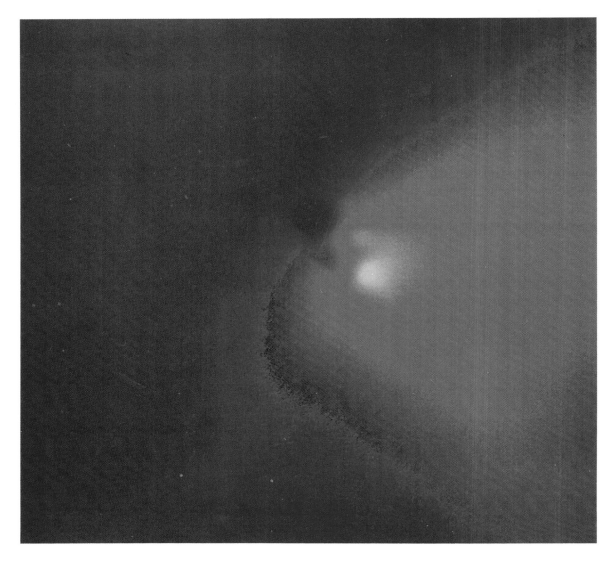

The nucleus of Halley's comet photographed by the Giotto spacecraft at a distance of 12,500 miles (20,000 kilometers).

and 1682 were all periodic returns of the same comet. He predicted that it would return again at the end of 1758 or the beginning of 1759. Halley died in 1742, so he missed seeing "his" comet return right on schedule, appearing in December, 1758, and reaching *perihelion* in March, 1759.

The oldest known report of Halley's Comet was made by a Chinese writer in 240 B.C. It appears on Babylonian clay tablets of 164 B.C. In 837 A.D., it came so close to Earth that its tail stretched almost from horizon to horizon. The Italian artist Giotto was so impressed when he saw it in 1301 that it became his model for the Star of Bethlehem in his great fresco of the Adoration of the Magi in Padua, Italy.

AN
ALLARM
TO
EUROPE:
By a Late Prodigious
COMET
ſeen November and December, 1680.

With a Predictive Diſcourſe. Together with ſome preceding and
ſome ſucceeding Cauſes of its ſad Effects to the *East* and
North Eastern parts of the World.

Namely, *ENGLAND*, *SCOTLAND*, *IRELAND*, *FRANCE*, *SPAIN*,
HOLLAND, *GERMANY*, *ITALY*, and many other places.

By *John Hill* Phyſitian and Aſtrologer.

The Form of the *COMET* with its Blaze or Stream as it was ſeen *December* the 24th.
Anno 1680. In the Evening.

London Printed by *H. Brugis* for *William Thackery* at the Angel in Duck-Lane

Comet Madness

In 1910, the world went comet-crazy. Even before Halley's Comet arrived, there was a display from another comet, called the Great Daylight Comet, which was

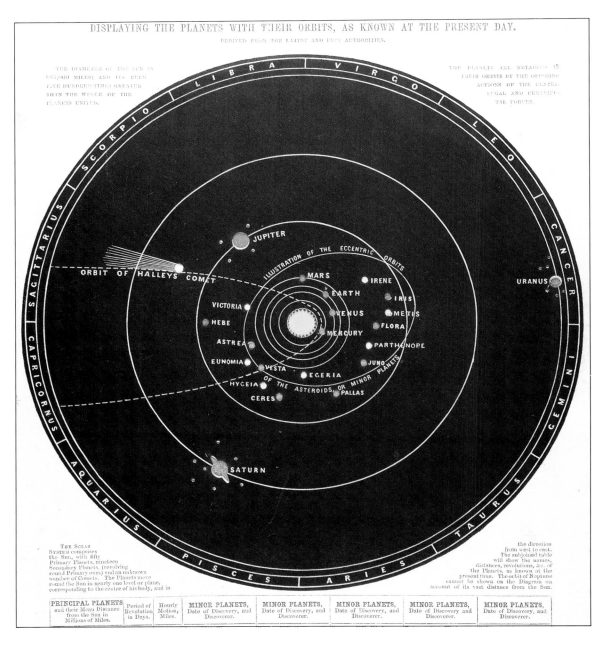

visible even in daylight skies. Then, Halley's Comet came close. There were constant newspaper stories, a rash of comet songs and sheet music, and a wide variety of comet jewelry and other mementos. There was also a mistaken, but widely publicized, theory that the comet's tail would inundate Earth with deadly cyanide gas. This rumor led to mass hysteria in many places. Frenzied populations stockpiled cylinders of oxygen, prayer meetings were held in preparation for

This educational diagram from 1857 shows the Sun at the center of the Solar System, together with the planets, the known asteroids, and the path of Halley's Comet as observed in 1835.

56

the end of the world, and there were a number of suicides.

Close Contact

By the time Halley's Comet next appeared, in 1986, space technology was so advanced that no less than five space probes were sent to intercept it and to try to photograph its nucleus.

The U.S.S.R.'s Vega 1 and Vega 2 came within 6,250 miles (10,000 kilometers) of the comet and took

The Giotto spacecraft took this picture of Halley's Comet from a distance of 11,000 miles (18,000 kilometers). The dark spot at the top left is the solid nucleus of the comet, estimated to be 9½ miles (15 kilometers) long and 5 miles (8 kilometers) across.

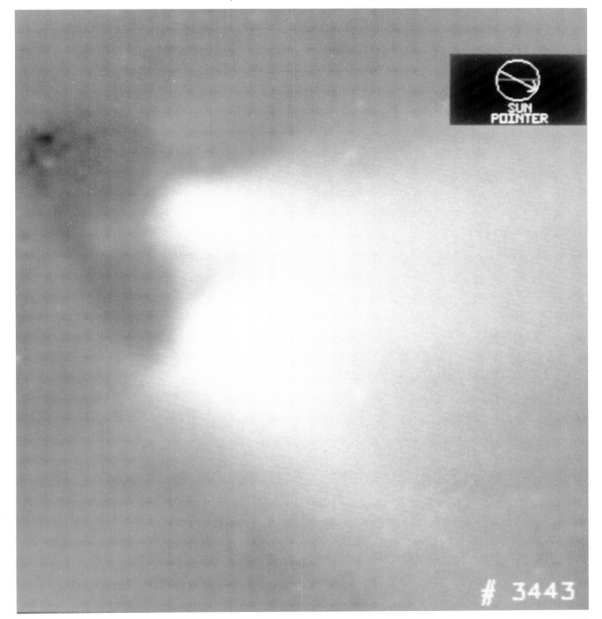

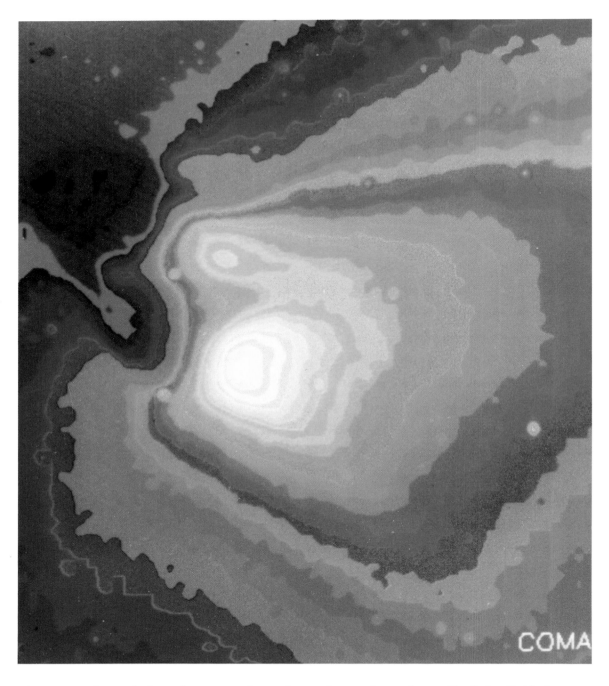

COMA

photographs of the dust-enveloped nucleus throwing out gas and dust. Two Japanese probes, Sakigake and Planet-A, came within 4,350,000 miles (7,000,000 kilometers) and 125,000 miles (200,000 kilometers) respectively. Most effective by far, though, was the European Space Agency's Giotto probe.

Giotto made a swift encounter with Halley's nucleus,

The Halley Multicolour Camera aboard the Giotto spacecraft took this image on March 13, 1986. The bright area below and to the right of the dark nucleus is a dust jet.

getting within 300 miles (500 kilometers) of it. Comet and probe passed one another at a relative speed of 42½ miles (68 kilometers) per second, or 156,000 mph (250,000 km/h). Giotto's instruments were badly damaged by dust impacts at this high velocity, but the probe confirmed what scientists had already guessed: the comet's nucleus is a lump of ice, darkened by thousands of years' exposure to cosmic radiation. Giotto took a close-up picture showing the nucleus as a dark, irregular lump measuring about 5 by 5 by 10 miles (8 by 8 by 16 kilometers).

Gradual Breakdown

Scientists calculate that comets passing through the inner Solar System lose about 0·1 percent of their mass, in the form of vapors and dust, on each orbit. That represents about 10,000,000 tons for the average comet, so that there would be nothing left after 1,000 orbits.

Comets are few and far between. A review in 1977 listed just 641 known comets, of which 108 were short-period and 533 long-period. Long-period comets sometimes appear once and are never seen again. They follow curved orbits which will project them out of the Solar System and on into the galaxy. Some comets break up and eventually disappear, leaving a ghostly orbit of particles to create an annual meteor shower if Earth coincides with it.

Endless Supply

There is no danger of running out of *cometary nuclei*, however. The Oort Cloud is an enormous stockpile of billions of "dirty snowballs" slowly circling the Sun. It is

Dust bands within the Solar System were discovered by IRAS near the inner edge of the Asteroid Belt. Comets lose an average of 10,000,000 tons of vapor and dust during each passage through the inner Solar System. Collisions with asteroids may also create dust and debris.

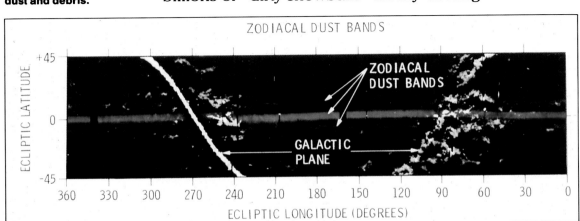

almost as if they are waiting for their turn to dive inward to the Solar System's inner regions where, for a brief spell, they can astound Earthbound observers with their glowing comas and streaming tails.

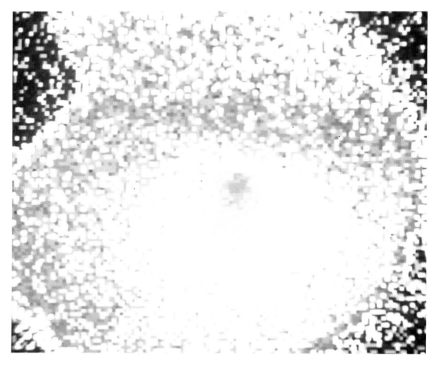

Comet IRAS-Araki-Alcock was a small comet that came exceptionally close to Earth in 1983. It was visible to the naked eye at one stage of its journey. This false-color image shows the brightest part of the comet as red, the coolest as blue.

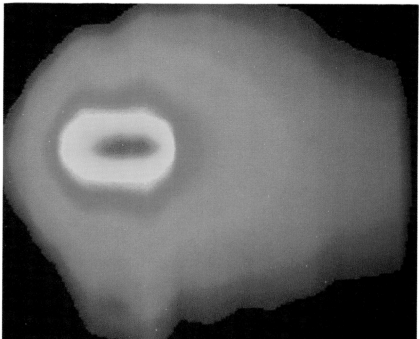

Comet IRAS-Araki- Alcock, imaged by the International Ultraviolet Explorer satellite, was shown to contain diatomic sulfur. This substance had never before been observed in comets. The image shows that the nucleus on the side facing the Sun, at lower left, is being vaporized more rapidly than the other side.

Books to Read

INTRODUCTORY READING

The Asteroids by Isaac Asimov (Gareth Stevens Inc., 1988)

Bright Stars, Red Giants and White Dwarfs by Melvin Berger (Putnam, 1983)

Comets by Franklyn M. Branley (Harper & Row Junior Books, 1987)

Comets and Meteors by Heather Couper (Franklin Watts, 1985)

Comets and Meteors by George S. Fichter (Franklin Watts, 1982)

Comets, Asteroids and Meteors by Dennis B. Fradin (Children's Press, 1984)

Comets, Meteors and Asteroids: Rocks in Space by David J. Darling (Dillon Press, 1984)

The Galaxies: Cities of Stars by David J. Darling (Dillon Press, 1985)

Halley: Comet 1986 by Franklyn M. Branley (Lodestar Books, 1983)

Halley's Comet by Norman D. Anderson & Walter R. Brown (Putnam, 1981)

Halley's Comet: What We've Learned by Gregory Vogt (Franklin Watts, 1987)

How Did We Find Out about Black Holes? by Isaac Asimov (Walker & Co., 1978)

How Did We Find Out about Comets? by Isaac Asimov (Walker & Co., 1975)

Voyagers from Space: Meteors and Meteorites by Patricia Lauber (Harper & Row Junior Books, 1989)

FURTHER READING

The Comet Handbook by Garry Stasiuk & Dwight Gruber (Stasiuk Enterprises, 1984)

Comets by Christopher O. Irwin (Mosaic Press, 1981)

Comets, Meteors and Asteroids: How They Affect Earth by Gibbilisco (TAB Books, 1985)

Cosmic Debris: Meteorites in History by John G. Burke (University of California Press, 1986)

Find a Falling Star by H. H. Nininger (Paul S. Eriksson, 1976)

Fire and Ice: A History of Comets in Art by Roberta J. Olsen (Walker & Co., 1985)

Handbook for Visual Meteor Observations edited by Paul Rogemans (Sky Publishing, 1989)

Maria Mitchell, First Lady of American Astronomy by Helen L. Morgan (Westminster/John Knox Press, 1977)

Meteor Showers by Gary W. Kronk (Enslow, 1988)

Meteorite Craters by Kathleen Mark (University of Arizona Press, 1987)

Meteorites and Their Parent Planets by Harry Y. McSween, Jr. (Cambridge University Press, 1987)

The Mystery of Comets by Fred L. Whipple (Smithsonian Institute Press, 1985)

Thunderstones and Shooting Stars: The Meaning of Meteorites by Robert S. Dodd (Harvard University Press, 1988)

The Ultimate Asteroid Book by Lee Lehman (Whitford Press, 1988)

Glossary

ABLATION Melting of the surface of, for example, an object entering Earth's atmosphere. The process dissipates the heat caused by air friction.

ACCRETION The process by which a body is built up by collisions with smaller bodies and particles.

ACID RAIN Rain containing a high concentration of acid, particularly sulfuric acid, owing to absorption of sulfur emissions from volcanic activity or industrial sources.

AMINO ACIDS Nitrogen-bearing acids, some of which form the basic structure of proteins.

AMOR ASTEROIDS A group of minor planets orbiting the Sun close to Earth, but outside Earth's orbit.

APHELION The point in a planet's orbit where it is furthest from the Sun.

APOLLO ASTEROIDS A group of minor planets that come inside Earth's orbit when they are closest to the Sun.

ASTEROID One of the thousands of minor planets in the Solar System, mostly under 62 miles (100 kilometers) in diameter.

ASTRONOMICAL UNIT (AU) A unit of measurement equal to the Earth's average distance from the Sun, about 93,000,000 miles (150,000,000 kilometers).

BASALT A dark rock associated with volcanic activity.

BINARY ASTEROID An asteroid that is accompanied by its own satellite.

BOLIDE An extremely bright meteor, which generally survives its passage through the Earth's atmosphere to strike the planet as a meteorite .

BRECCIA Rock fragments held together in a fine-grained material.

CARBONACEOUS METEORITE A meteorite of primitive matter including organic carbon compounds.

CHONDRULE A small sphere of silicate material, which possibly condensed in the original solar nebula 4,600,000,000 years ago.

COMA The visible gaseous halo around the nucleus of a comet.

COMET A body that orbits the Sun, usually with an eccentric orbit. When a comet is visible from Earth, it trails a tail of gas and dust.

COMETARY NUCLEUS The solid center of a comet, usually several miles in diameter, made of ice and dust.

CRETACEOUS PERIOD The period on Earth from about 135,000,000 to about 66,000,000 years ago, when life was dominated by reptiles.

ECCENTRIC ORBIT An orbit that is not circular.

ECLIPTIC The circle where the plane of Earth's orbit meets the celestial sphere.

FLUORESCENCE The emission of visible light radiation from an outside radiation source, such as sunlight.

INCANDESCENCE The emission of visible light radiation due to an increase in temperature.

IONIZED GAS A gas in which the atoms have been electrically charged, usually by intense heat or radiation.

LIGHT-YEAR The distance traveled by a ray of light in one year in a vacuum: 63,240 Astronomical Units.

MARE BASIN Dark areas, particularly on the Moon, where volcanic lavas once flowed to form "seas" bounded by higher features.

METEOR A body from space that burns up when it enters the atmosphere of Earth or another planet .

METEORITE A body from space that passes through a planet's atmosphere and strikes the planet.

METEOROID A piece of solid matter moving through space, which is seen as a meteor if it enters Earth's atmosphere, and is called a meteorite if it reaches the surface of Earth or any other planet.

METEOR SHOWER A regular annual profusion of meteors as Earth passes through the orbit of a dead comet and encounters its dust.

MINOR PLANET A small body within the Solar System, most of which orbit the Sun within the Asteroid Belt between the orbits of Mars and Jupiter.

OORT CLOUD The theoretical spherical cloud of cometary nuclei which forms the gravitational boundary of the Solar System.

PERIHELION The point in a planet's orbit where it is closest to the Sun.

PLANETOID A minor planet or asteroid.

RADIANT The point from which all meteors from a particular shower appear to come.

RETROGRADE ORBIT A clockwise orbital motion, as seen from the north pole of a planet. Most Solar System orbits are counterclockwise.

SILICATE A rock composed partly of silicon and oxygen, together with metallic oxides.

SONIC BOOM The noise of the shockwave from objects traveling faster than the speed of sound.

SPECTROGRAPH An instrument used to photograph the spectra of light and other radiation.

SPECTRUM A spread of different wavelengths of electromagnetic radiation, such as the colors of white light dispersed by a prism.

TERTIARY PERIOD The period on Earth between about 65,000,000 and 2,000,000 years ago, in which mammals became dominant.

TSUNAMI A giant tidal wave caused by a volcanic eruption or some other cataclysmic event.

Index